# MY LIFE IN MOMENTS

## A Poetic Memoir

Jessica Amos

Praise for MY LIFE IN MOMENTS

"Jessica Amos' debut memoir shakes out like a polaroid in hand… a revelation in form and function that is both unique and universally profound."
**–Robyn Saunders-Wilson, author of *Junkyard Princess***

"Amos' visceral imagery takes you by the hand… sharing secrets, trusting them in your care, and you leave feeling the weight of an invisible friendship bracelet she sneakily tied around your wrist."
**–Katie Gilmour, author of *This Changes Everything, This Changes Nothing***

"Jessica's writing lingers in that beautiful, in-between space where memories are fragmented and tender, leaving room for curiosity, wonder, and imagination to unfold."
**–Jocelyn Fitzgerald, author of *Creative Art Therapies***

"All I could think of was Jessica's sweet, happy little face and I had an overwhelming urge to use roses and fancy cakes from the 70s… so that's what I did."
**–Danielle Krysa, cover artist and author of *Creative Block***

For
Haven and Brannock

# PRELUDE

Your parents were young.
Only sixteen and eighteen
when they had your sister.
You arrived a year later.

They were always so stylish.
You would watch them
dancing in the living room,
showing you the latest moves.

You were beautiful.
He called you his *Playboy Bunny*.
You didn't like that.

At age 12
you started smoking and drinking.
You would steal sips of liquor
during your parents' parties.

It was a drawing
of a flower.

You won first prize.
You didn't call yourself an artist.

Your first time
was at a friend's house
during lunch hour.
It wasn't good.
It wasn't special.

You picked the pattern,
bought the fabric
worked hard,
made an original.
You wore it to school,
and felt proud.

A week later,
a girl showed up
wearing the same thing.

She had found the exact
pattern and fabric.
Imitation was not flattery.

Anorexia.
It was your way
of having control
over something.
Anything.

You were abducted.
From a street corner.
The cops said
it was your fault
for wearing a halter
and cutoffs.

Drugs numbed the pain.
Temporal happiness.
You weren't so shy
and friendless.

Too many lovers to count.
Too many abortions.

Better to not think.
Not to feel.

Heroin helped.

He was funny and charismatic.
You were quiet and shy.

You came from California money.
He came from dirt floor Oklahoma.
Both with equal anguish.

He was handsome.
Dark hair.
Clear blue eyes.
Infectious smile.
Magnetic.

You got married,
and fixed up houses.

He wasn't always reliable.
But he was handy.

You wanted a baby more than anything.

He only had *one* testicle.
Couldn't have kids.

You tried anyway.

Turns out,
turkey basters
are for more
than just turkeys.

She was a miracle baby.

You got clean to have her.
You stayed clean.
For a while.

You ran the stairs
to induce labor.
She arrived on May 9.
Her due date.

She was chubby.
Smiley. Happy.
You couldn't stop
kissing her.

You were smiley
and happy too.

He drank a lot.
He threw a two-by-four
at your head.
You were holding the baby
and turned to protect her.

It hit your arm instead.

You came home.
He wasn't there.
But the baby was.

He left her home alone.

He was drunk.
The car crashed.

He died instantly.

He carried a picture
of his baby girl
in his wallet.

You were raped
while she was asleep
in your room.

You didn't want to wake her,
so you kept quiet
and took it.

You and the baby
lived in a car
for a while.

You left her
at the babysitter
for several days.

You knew she was safe
while you got high.

Prison took you
from her.

Identity theft.

Your parents took her in.

The separation rang
in your hearts.

Jesus saved you.
He forgave you.
He loved you.

Three years later,
you were released.

New life waited for you.
*She* waited for you.

# ACT ONE

First Memories:
My room.
The garden.
The greenhouse.
The river.
My ducky pillow.
Breakfast.
Trips to Mexico.
Neighborhood friends.
Bedtime.

Stability.

You built me a swing
by the river's edge,
between two tall trees.

Forward swing,
fly over the water.
Suspended
above the current.
Weightless.
Timeless.

We ate Rocky Road
and watched the Cosby Show.
You put me to sleep,
tracing my face
with your index finger.

That was my favorite.

We left for Mexico
in the middle of the night.

You carried me,
half asleep, to the plane.
I slept most of the way.

We lived in a trailer
on the beach.
It was hot.
You caught *huge* fish.
My cabbage patch kid
lost its shoe.

You took tap classes
at the Rec Center.
I begged to go with you.
The answer: always no.
I imagined you
having the best time.

You brought back dolls:

Irish.
Dutch.
Spanish.
Indian.
African.
Mexican.

You had shark jaws
on the basement walls.
Some big. Some small.
They were awesome.
I couldn't look away.

I watched you
slaughter a cow,
pulling its insides out
with your bare hands!
Intestines, bowels, stomach.
All while eating
an egg salad sandwich.
I don't like egg salad.

Your brewery was huge.
Both light and dark.
There was a small table
between ceiling-high
drums of beer.

We ate lunch there.
It smelled like wood
and yeast and hops.
Permeating everything.

I was pretending
the box was a boat;
pulling myself
around the living room,
legs sticking out.
My knee shipwrecked
on the brick fireplace.
Blood was everywhere.
I still have the scar.

*"I lick all my food
before I eat it."*
An old military habit.
I believed you,
and stopped stealing
your pickles.

Constant rain.
Everything green.
Giant garden.
Slugs everywhere.
Victorian house.
Quilt-covered beds.

A blue plastic tea set.
My favorite.

Your bureau:
a wonderland.

Jewelry.
Perfume.
Lotion.

My sneaky hands
touching everything.

I didn't know you,
but I was sure
I would recognize you.
Instinctively.

I had a photo of you
that I took with me,
*just in case*.

It was strange
not knowing you,
not recognizing you.

Most kids
*know* their mother.

I didn't live with you
right away.
We needed time
to adjust.

You stayed in a room
above the garage
with a mini fridge
and a big bed.

You were really nice.
I knew you'd be a good mom.

You met at a group
for ex-convicts.
Both of you released
six months apart,
both born again in prison...
recovered heroin addicts...

Stories too similar
to ignore.

(He was barely 18
when he was arrested
for armed robbery.

San Quentin Prison
in California.

He was good looking.
Sensitive.
You can only imagine
what that was like.)

When I first lived with you,
I slept on a cot in the pantry.
The winter frost blew in
through the window casing.
Mice lived there too.
I didn't like it.

He built a bunk bed for my room –
much better than the pantry.
I built a castle
out of Kleenex boxes:
*She-Ra's Castle.*

Mice made nests in my shoes.
I was scared to put them on.

I had a nightmare,
and called for you.

You came to my room
butt naked.
*He* was sleeping over.
That was the first
(and last)
time I called for you.

I wet the bed.
*He* was sleeping over again.
I didn't want to wake you,
So, I changed my clothes,
pulled the wet sheets off the bed,
and slept on the bare mattress.

You got pregnant out of wedlock.
As new Christians,
you had to make it right.
Marriage was the only solution.

You slipped on the ice.
I was only six,
But I caught you
before you hit the ground.
You told me I saved the baby.
I felt really proud.

The day you were born,
he took me horseback riding.
My horse wouldn't cross the stream.
We had to turn around.
It was O.K.
I couldn't wait to meet you.

I took you to school
for *Show and Tell*.
My little brother:
the cutest baby ever.

I loved watching you
sew your wedding dress.
So much lace, so beautiful.

"*You're not the boss of me.*"
I thought you should know.

After the wedding, you said:
"Now *I'm the boss of you.*"

You meant to be funny.
But I was serious.

Everything changed.
I had a new Mom.
A new Dad.
A new Home.
A new Brother.
Things I never had before.

I knew without knowing.
We were different.
Shame covered our household.
Few people were allowed in.
I didn't question why.

You felt like an outsider...
angry, hurt, scared.
Prison will do that to you.
I expected you to have answers.
In a lot of ways,
we raised each other.

We went to church a lot.
I liked the songs and bible stories.
You told me I was born a sinner.

You were the best spot
to play in the yard.
You witnessed all my childhood joy.
With you I was a mommy,
a spy, an explorer.
I was everything.
I was magic.

You were my hiding place
when they were fighting.
I found comfort
in your old coats and dresses.
Hanging. Forgotten.
You muffled the sounds.
Sometimes I fell asleep.

You called me a jerk
for not doing what you wanted.
I was only nine.
It made me hurt physically,
like I'd been punched.
We stopped being friends.

You taught me new drawing styles,
and mailed little cassette tapes
with recordings you made.
You sang songs to me,
and told stories.
You wrote me a book
about a stowaway mouse.
You were *interested* in me.

I invited Jesus into my heart.

You assured me:
It *wasn't* about understanding.
It was about faith.

You were two gigantic lilac trees
in the front yard –
tops all grown together.
Like two lovers
who couldn't stay apart.
I was the child in between you.

You had her cornered,
slamming the door into her body.
I flew from my hiding place –
heart pounding in my ears –
hurling my small form at yours.
In a flash, you slammed me
into the wall.
I never interfered again.

You weren't the first person
to leave me in the backseat
while you rode upfront with your mom.
I hated when friends did that.
It was always so lonely
and uncomfortable.

To this day you are
my ultimate delight.
I lose myself in you for hours.
Time stands still.

We were in the check-out line.
I was still on the fence
about calling you *Dad*.
I tried it out:
"*Dad*," I said.
You didn't seem to notice.
I called you *Dad* after that.
Hoping eventually you'd notice.

You came in the best colors,
and smelled like fruit.
Coloring with cherry
was my favorite.

Sunday School:
The movie was called *Left Behind*.
It took place after the rapture.
Christians were being beheaded.
A child with a red balloon
was led to the guillotine.
There was a slicing sound.
The balloon floated into the sky.

We were terrified.

How to explain the safety of you?
I had to crawl
on hands and knees
to your center.
A delightful shelter.
Dark and light.
Warm and cool.
Floral and musky.

The entire school population
was out on the grass.
Girls doing cartwheels,
boys playing soccer.
A ball kicked sideways as
I rounded into a cartwheel.
KICK!
The ball flew across the field
into the bushes.
Everyone cheered!

I hid in the closet
until I heard the door slam.
That's when I knew it would be over.
You found me and knew my plan:
Bags packed, ready to run.
Where would I have gone anyway?

You were the first person
to tell me about sex.
We were in second grade.
You had heard the details
from your older brother.
That's what I think of
when I remember you.

You would sit on one another's laps,
braiding each other's hair...
whispering secrets.
You would giggle,
comfortable with such intimacy.
I wasn't that sort of girl.
But I wanted to be.

I pretended the wall was you,
pressing myself into your arms.
You held me and told me you loved me.
You apologized for not being there.
I wished you hadn't died.

I hope you felt more comfortable
with me next to you.
I didn't want you to feel alone
in the backseat.

We collected tadpoles
in a bucket
and forgot about them.
Soon the vents started to "ribbit."
They croaked for days.
Literally and figuratively.

You took us out to Chinese food,
and rented a house.
We had so much fun together.
Just the three of us.
I didn't want to go home.
But when the fight was over,
we went back.

Going to your house was a lesson
on *how to be a girl.*
We wore matching outfits.
Your mom curled our hair.
You did my make-up.
We choreographed dance routines
to *Wilson Phillips*
and *Paula Abdul.*

It was my favorite outfit:
Matching tie-dyed leggings
and oversized t-shirt.
The roller skates
(that fit onto my sneakers)
were the pièce de résistance

You immortalized the moment
with a picture.
Thank you.

After you fought,
I would find you
in your room crying.
I comforted you
as best a child can.
I never cried.
You cried for us all.

My socks slipped on the ladder
as I climbed into your loft.
Falling, my head hit
the dresser corner.
Blood everywhere.
Your mom held me in the backseat
as we drove to the hospital.
Thirteen stitches later,
I was never invited over again.

It was the only time
you got *really* mad at me.
I would have been too.
To watch your kid
throw her lunch in the trash.
*Right in front of you!*
As if you didn't have better things
to do than make her lunch.

Your house:

Fragrant leis.
Floral muumuus.
Ocean views.
Elegance.
Mangos.
Geckos.
Beauty.

You.

Hawaii.

You were all over the yard.
Spring meant procreation.
We'd throw you against the house,
trying to separate your bodies.
You never let go of each other.

*Grasshoppers.*

I kept out of the way.
Quiet.
Invisible.
In constant apology.

Summer was for
*Anne of Green Gables*
and *Anne of Avonlea*.
She taught me of bosom friends
and kindred spirits.
I knew someday I would find mine.

You would doodle on a notepad
while talking on the phone.

I do the same thing now.
Even my doodles look like yours.

When we brought you home,
you hid in the closet.
So scared.
I held you, whispering comforts,
until you felt safe.
After that you slept in my room.
You were a good dog.

The only predictable thing
was unpredictability.
I became an expert
at reading moods.

You went all-out at Christmas.
Spending hours shopping
for the perfect gifts.
Your excitement was contagious.
I loved seeing you happy.
You had a really great laugh.

We built a fort in your room,
between the bed and the dresser.
We used random objects
to hold the blankets in place.
Our cozy cave became chaos
when the cat started jumping.
Your ghetto blaster fell on my head.
I kept yelling, *"Brain damage!"*
A huge purple goose egg
graced my forehead for a week.

I asked God to save me
every night at bedtime.
I asked forgiveness.
For what? I wasn't sure.
I just knew I needed it.

You'd sing:
*"Hey good lookin'.*
*What you got cookin'?*
*Hows 'bout cookin'*
*something up with me?"*

Then you kissed her.
That was good.

The tickets were cheaper,
if I lied and said I was twelve.
I wore jeans and sorrels,
and was soaked after 10 minutes.
By the end of the day,
I was hooked on snowboarding.

I sat in my living room.
Bags packed.
Waiting.
I called you.
Your sister said,
*"She's in the bath".*
You didn't call back.
You never came.
Our friendship was over.

The first day of Eighth Grade:
You were the only person
I knew in homeroom.
We had every class together that year.
We were best friends
all through High School.

You were there the first time I smoked pot –
so cool and so much older.
Months later you died
during a routine operation.

The whole school showed up
for your funeral.
It was open casket.
I couldn't bring myself to look.

I wanted to be a cheerleader.
But I was very bad at it.
I wore jeans under my skirt,
and got stoned
with the coach's daughter.
A month later, I quit.

You picked a fight with me
in the hall during passing period.
A large crowd formed.
*"You prance around like
you own the place,"* you sneered.

I left you standing there.
No satisfaction
of a reaction from me.

I went to a party
and lied about it.
I was grounded
for two weeks –
no friends, no tv,
no phone calls.
I sewed vintage buttons
all over my Jansport.

It was the only time
I cried in front of you.
I don't remember the details.
Except that you had yelled.
I didn't cry again
until I was 25.

When *Kurt Cobain* died,
I snuck over to Gina's house.
We sat in the kitchen,
listening to his music.
We drank tequila
and cried.

I woke up in my sleeping bag
on your living room floor.
Disoriented.
Remembering where I was,
I threw my head back down.
The corner of my eye
Hit the brick fireplace.
I almost lost my eye.

You invited me to stay
for the Summer.
Three months of Art College.
I was beyond excited.
My parents said No.
I was too young
LA was too corrupt,
too dangerous.

It was the only time
you didn't fight.
It made me uneasy
to see you happy.
But I loved it.

I got good at lying.
I lied about everything.
Even things that didn't
require lies.

My friends didn't like you.
But I wanted *them* to like *me*.
So, I wrote a cruel note
with your name on it.
You gave it to a teacher.
I was suspended for a week.
I'm still sorry.

You didn't stop me
from dressing like a boy…
giant skater pants.
You even tried them on
one time as a joke.
You were funny.
When you wanted to be.

Two boys were in the pool.
I felt self-conscious.
Would it be weird to lay out
with my clothes on?

Yes.

My bikini top snapped
as I lifted my shirt off.
The boys were laughing.
I was totally exposed.
The only thing worse?
Running away in shame.
I was mortified,
but I stayed.

Vacation.
We were at our best as a family.
It was good.

I loved the sand
and the crashing waves.
I even ran on the beach.
Light, free.
You laughed to see me run.
It made you happy
to see me happy.

You told me sex was bad,
and boys only wanted one thing.
- that it was my fault
if boys *lusted* after me.
But I *loved* boys,
and they loved *me*.
So I kissed them *all*,
but never more.

*"Is Mom there?"*
You pressed me to tell you
why I was calling.

*"I started my period."*

Oh.
We were both sorry you asked.

It was titled *Traffic*.
You gave me an A+
for the entire year
because it was so good.

You believed in me.
But you also liked
to be inappropriate
with your female students.

Eventually,
you were fired for it.

Aardvark's,
Haight Street,
San Francisco.

I bought:
Army green polyester pants.
Chartreuse cardigan.
Floral polyester shirt
(with the big collar).

Very 70s, very *grandpa chic*.
Perfect with socks
and Birkenstock's.

You knew a shortcut
through the woods.
Why wouldn't I trust you?
We were cousins.

Cousins by marriage.
Step-cousins.
You tried to rape me.
It was your first time
trying something like that.
Fortunate for me.
But not so fortunate
for the girls that came later.

You knocked me down.

I was on all fours,
trying to crawl away.
You had my pant leg.
The green polyester ones.
I screamed at you,
"*Are you trying to rape me?!?*"
That surprised you.

But you still had me.
So, I let you
Fondle my boobs.

God, you were gross.

You asked me not to tell anyone.
Who was I going to tell?
It was probably my fault
for leading you on.

I dyed my hair black.
You told me I looked
like a whore.

You lit my fucking hair on fire.
On purpose.

Asshole.

I was 14.
You were my *biggest* crush.

Our first kiss
was the *French* kind.
It took me by surprise,
but after that
I was hooked.

Rolling Stone Magazine
was my favorite.
My walls were covered
from floor to ceiling
with the big square pages.

The *Doors, Nirvana, Metallica...*
I wasn't allowed
to listen to their music,
but I loved them all.

I met you at the bus stop.
You offered a tab of acid.
You were cute,
so I figured, *why not?*

I went missing that day.

You grounded me
for going missing.
I tried to stop smiling.
Everything seemed funny.

Later, when I was alone
in my room,
the hallucinations
weren't so funny.

It made me self-conscious
how you watched me during PE.
Like maybe you hated me.
Until I realized,
it wasn't *hate*,
it was lust.

You were watching my body.
Not *me*.

You bought me a snowboard.
It cost a lot,
*plus* all the gear.

I knew it was your way of saying
"*I love you.*"

You taught me how to smoke,
and look cool doing it.

I still smoke cigarettes,
and on occasion
it reminds me of you.

It was our first time
hanging out.
We went to the indoor pool.
You had sex
with a random guy there.
Later that night,
we went to a party.
Afterward, you kissed me
on the lips.
I didn't want to seem prude,
so I kissed you back.

We met you at Safeway.
So cute,
and so much older.
You invited us to a party
at your house that night.

Of course we were going.

We snuck out
through the dog door.
We carried rocks
as weapons.
We hitched a ride,
with pro snowboarders.

They invited us to *their* party.
But we already had plans.

We lied about our age.
I said I was sixteen.
We got drunk and stoned.
I could have lost my virginity.
But I wasn't ready.
He was nice about it.


We made it back
through the dog door,
just before sunrise.

You found *all* my mixed tapes...
the ones I had painstakingly
recorded off the radio.

It required *hours*
of stealth and work...
hitting RECORD every time
a good song came on.

You threw them all away
and turned me over to Satan.

I understood why
you were protective.

You didn't understand:
I wasn't you.

We didn't share the same fears.
Mainly, you had them.
I didn't.

We couldn't be friends
anymore.
I was a Christian now.
*For real.*
You all moved on.


I cried at night
from the ache
of missing you.

I could stay out
as long as I wanted.
No one asked questions.
In your mind,
*Youth Group* kids
were *good kids*.
Even the bad ones.

The freedom felt
*soooo* good.

I threw it all away:
Old Levi 501's.
Vintage sweaters.
Concert t-shirts.
My Birkenstock's.

I started shopping
at The Gap.

Women's Retreats.
They were "our thing".
We needed that.

I was on my knees.
A dozen of you
laying hands on me.
All praying
in strange languages.
You told me to
talk like a baby.

"Goo-goo, *gah-gah*," I said.

I thought something was wrong
with me because I didn't
have the gift of
*speaking in tongues.*

Summer was for
babysitting you.
You'd play outside,
I'd watch tv.
Sometimes we'd take
the trolly
to the beach.

I was tired of lying,
so I answered honestly.
It didn't go well.
You lectured me
for an hour.
My plans got canceled.
I stuck to lies after that.

You were good
at apologizing.

I was good
at forgiveness.

Your daily:
Wake at 5am…
make coffee,
read the Bible,
pray.

Make breakfast,
pack lunches,
drop off kids,
clean 5-10 houses,
go grocery shopping,
volunteer at the prison,
laundry, dinner, kids,

Go to bed by 10pm.

You said I was depressed.
Was I?

You were really worried.

I didn't feel a thing.

You tried talking to me.
But it was too late.
So many parts of me,
already shut down.
I didn't know how
to talk to you.
Not safely.

This hurt your feelings.
It wasn't personal,
it was protection.

We performed at juvenile facilities
and homeless shelters.

I wondered:
Did the juvie kids accept Christ
out of sincerity?
Or were they just afraid
of being dragged into hell,
kicking and screaming,
like the play implied?

At the homeless shelter,
men would jerk off in the front row.

It's hard to know the impact we had.

I ripped all the pages out.
All the hatred
and anger.
All the promises
I made to myself.

Promises to grow up
and be different
from *you*.

Food still on my plate,
I wasn't hungry.
You said it was a waste,
an abomination.

You turned me over to Satan.

You were nice about it,
but if I didn't try harder,
you would have to fire me.

You single handedly
improved my work ethic.

Things didn't add up.
No one seemed to notice.

I kept all questions to myself.

You fell asleep
during a prayer circle.

When we nudged you awake,
you said,
*"I was deep in prayer."*

You were instantly
one of my favorite people.

I'd heard it before.
When people first met me,
they thought I was a bitch.

You said I acted
like a rich snob.
I laughed.

That's rich!

God told you
I had the gift of healing.

You led me to her,
so I could pray
over her.

The next day,
her injury was healed.
Completely gone.

Very impressive.

"When I die,
I want to be cremated.
I want my ashes scattered
off a cliff by the ocean.
I know it sounds cliché,
but I want to be remembered
in a place full of life.
I want you to walk any shore
and remember me."

To which you said:
"That's an abomination."

You showed me your penis.
Right there
in the coffee shop.
It was pierced.
You wanted me
to touch it.
But I didn't.

Art class.
My favorite.

After graduation,
you delivered a gift:
A sketch book.

On the inside cover you wrote:

"*Never stop drawing.
Someday your sketchbook
might be worth something.
Like da Vinci's.*"

I told you
what you wanted to hear.
Of course you were surprised.
You didn't really know me.
How could you?
Not even I knew me.

# ACT TWO

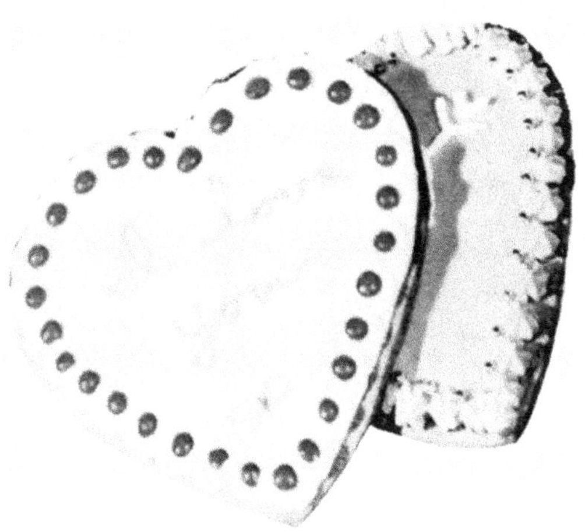

I was serving coffee
when you walked in...

Grungy.
Snowboarder.
Older.
Nonchalant.
Quiet.
Magnetic.

We talked.
We flirted.
We played coy.
We fell in love.

It was a whirlwind.

You said I was beautiful.
The way you looked at me
when you said it.
I believed you.
You saw me.

I felt sick
(and wanted to flee),
but forced myself
to stay in your arms.
It might be my only
chance for love.


It was a risk.
I let you love me.

Your love
taught me to love –
brought me out of hiding.

I was ravenous for more.

If sex was a sin,
then I was going to hell!

I had tasted the fruit
of orgasmic passion.

I still felt like *me*,
only more alive.

Who knew?!
Sex was **good**!

We decided to get married.
I didn't tell them.
They heard it
from someone else.

Not good.

I was nineteen.
My wedding day.
They were against it.
I didn't care.
I loved you.
You were the *One*.

Our love was strong.
We followed the rules –
did what was expected.
We could have continued
like that.
But not really.

You saved my life –
so small and helpless.
Something split wide open
inside my heart.

*Goosh!*

All those promises
I had made?

They were for *you*.

But first, I had to *give*
those promises to *myself*.

So I did.

I started thinking:

This is *my* life.
M I N E.
I can't keep looking to others
for who I am.

I need to figure out *who I am*.


(Shit)

Who was I?

No one could tell me.

I reached into my past.
Faced it.
Felt it.
Forgave it.

Found myself there.

With shame,
I recounted the events
of the past week.

The events of a lifetime.

You looked me in the eyes and said,
"*You know that's not okay. Right?*"

"Yes," I said.
"*I shouldn't have done that.*"

"No," you said.
"*What he did wasn't right.
You did nothing wrong.*"

No one ever told me that:

*It wasn't my fault.*

I didn't lie this time.

"*You hurt me.*"

I needed
time and space.
Years. A Lifetime.

I isolated myself.

To hear my own voice.
No external input.

Night after night,
my fingers flew
across the keyboard.

I wrote for
the girl, abandoned;
the girl, scared;
the girl, ashamed;
the girl, alone;
the girl, depressed;
the girl with no tears.

I wrote for my*self*.

I taught myself to cry.
It took years.

Eventually the sobs came,
for the first time
in a decade;
at age 25.

I cried for
the loss,
the fear,
the shame,
the secrets,
the loneliness.

Myself.

I held you,
and cried.

Your unprotected innocence,
a reflection of my own.

Your warmth and light –
the ultimate healing salve.

Recovered losses:

Music.
Swearing.
Cigarettes.
Laughter.
Vintage.
501's.

I watched you...
your tenderness
and patience
with our children.

A new context:
*loving Father*.

Dark bedroom.
I was crying,
again, because
I hated myself.

Then it came to me:
Hatred is tiring.
Exhausting.

*I will love myself.*

I told my young self:
"*You are loved.*
*You are valid.*
*You are seen.*
*You are beautiful.*
*You are smart.*
*You light up a room.*
*You are not alone.*
*I am here now.*
*You. Are. LOVED.*"

Endlessly.
Absolutely.
Exuberantly.

LOVED.

You said:
"We're all doing the best we can
with what we've been given."

That became my mantra.
For myself,
for others.

Forgiveness was inevitable.

Forgiveness for
you, me, all of it.

# POSTLUDE

Every moment...
a lifetime,
an eternity.

And that's how
we make our way
to the end.

Moment to moment,
eternity to eternity.

It was a bowling alley.
Of all places.

I was bursting
with *joy*,
and gratitude.

Where did it come from?
So sudden and eager.

It was always here,
always mine.

This story is not me,
But it's also not *not* me.

Shaped in every moment,
remembered and forgotten.

If not for suffering,
I wouldn't know compassion.

If not for pain,
I wouldn't know healing.

If not for limits,
I wouldn't know freedom.

If not for fear,
I wouldn't know peace.

If not for shame,
I wouldn't know love.

If not for mistakes,
I wouldn't know humor.


If not for sadness,
I wouldn't know joy.


If not for hate,
I wouldn't know forgiveness.


If not for control,
I wouldn't know acceptance.

# THE END

(but not really)

**JESSICA AMOS** is a writer and artist. This is her first book but not her last. She lives in Salem, Oregon, and online at www.staywithyourself.com.

**MY LIFE IN MOMENTS** was originally written in 2013, and left to gather digital dust in Jessica's writing archives... until now.

Just as we change over time, so do our memories (and motivations). Who's to say why we remember the things we do, and forget others? What evidence is there that what we remember is how things actually happened? And even more confounding, how is it that the stories and memories told to us by those who came before us, somehow become our own?

Memories are rarely chronological – they come and go as they please, always slightly changed since their last visit. This poetic memoir serves to explore the gaps *between events* as much as the events themselves. Names, places, and timelines are mentioned loosely, or not at all, to give a 'snapshot' effect to the moments.

www.ingramcontent.com/pod-product-compliance
Lightning Source LLC
Chambersburg PA
CBHW051519150726
47997CB00001B/312